LRN

Renewals
01159 293388
www.bromley.gov.uk/libraries

Bromley
THE LONDON BOROUGH
www.bromley.gov.uk

Please return/renew this item
by the last date shown.
Books may also be renewed by
phone and Internet.

Animals on the...
Farm

Siân Smith

Raintree

Raintree is an imprint of Capstone Global Library Limited, a company incorporated in England and Wales having its registered office at 7 Pilgrim Street, London, EC4V 6LB – Registered company number: 6695582

www.raintreepublishers.co.uk
myorders@raintreepublishers.co.uk

Text © Capstone Global Library Limited 2015
First published in hardback in 2014
The moral rights of the proprietor have been asserted.

Edited by Siân Smith, John-Paul Wilkins and Helen Cox Cannons
Designed by Cynthia Akiyoshi
Picture research by Mica Brancic and Tracy Cummins
Production by Victoria Fitzgerald
Originated by Capstone Global Library
Printed and bound in China

ISBN 978 1 406 28051 7
18 17 16 15 14
10 9 8 7 6 5 4 3 2 1

British Library Cataloguing in Publication Data
A full catalogue record for this book is available from the British Library.

Acknowledgements
We would like to thank the following for permission to reproduce photographs: Shutterstock pp. 1 (© Lynne Carpenter), 2 (© Erik Lam), 3 left (© ignatius 63), 3 middle, 20 top right (© Eric Isselee), 3 right (© kontur-vid), 4 (© risteski goce), 5 (© Levranii), 6 (© Fotokostic), 7 (© PCHT), 8 (© Nancy Kennedy), 9 (© Helga Chirk), 10 (© azure), 11 (© Mark O'Flaherty), 12 (© Krisztina Farkas), 13 (© Nancy Hochmuth), 14 (© imagesbycat), 15, 22b (© mnapoli), 16 (© Heiko Kiera), 17 (© CreativeNature.nl), 18 (© Stargazer), 19, 22a (© Ruud Morijn Photographer), 20 bottom left (© Tsekhmister), 20 bottom right (© Aaron Amat), 20 top left (© MaZiKab), 21 (© smereka).

Front cover photograph of a Jersey cow reproduced with kind permission of Shutterstock (© Andrzej Wilusz).

Every effort has been made to contact copyright holders of material reproduced in this book. Any omissions will be rectified in subsequent printings if notice is given to the publisher.

Contents

Farm animals

I can see a cow.

I can see a rabbit.

I can see a hen.

I can see a cockerel.

I can see a donkey.

pig

I can see a pig.

sheep

I can see a sheep.

I can see a dog.

I can see a cat.

horse

I can see a horse.

I can see a goat.

turkey

I can see a turkey.

I can see a rat.

I can see a mouse.

duck

I can see a duck.

I can see a goose.

Farm quiz

Which animals live on a farm?

tiger

horse

hen

meerkat

Answer: Horses and hens live on a farm.

What am I?

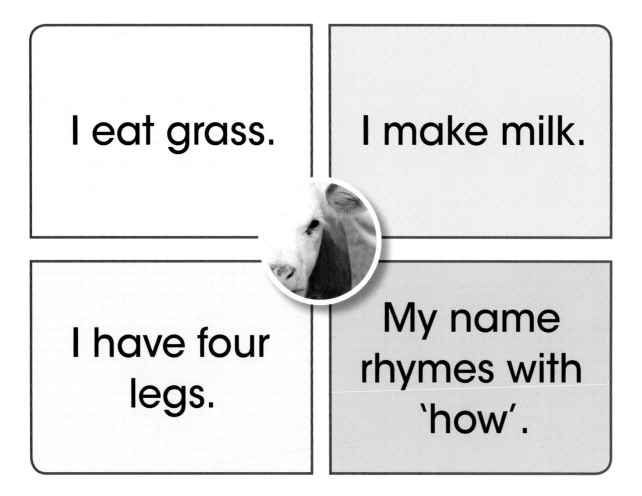

I eat grass.

I make milk.

I have four legs.

My name rhymes with 'how'.

Picture glossary

 goose

 turkey

Index

Notes for teachers and parents

Before reading

Tuning in: Talk about farm animals the child has seen. Talk about baby animals and their special names.

After reading

Recall and reflection: What is a baby horse called? What is a baby cow called?

Sentence knowledge: Help the child to count the number of words in each sentence.

Word knowledge (phonics): Encourage the child to point at the word 'can' on any page. Sound out the phonemes in the word "c/a/n". Ask the child to sound out each letter as they point at it and then blend the sounds together to make the word "can".

Word recognition: Challenge the child to race you to point at the word 'I' on any page.

Rounding off

Learn the following rhyme:

The turkey is a funny bird,
His head goes wobble, wobble
("wobble" head forwards and backwards like a turkey)
And all he knows is just one word...
And that is GOBBLE-GOBBLE!

Word coverage

Sentence stem

I can see a _____.

High-frequency words

a
can
I
see

**Ask children to read
these words:**

cockerel   p7
hen   p6
pig   p9
rabbit   p5

Topic words

cat
cockerel
cow
dog
donkey
duck
goat
goose
hen
horse
mouse
pig
rabbit
rat
sheep
turkey